IMAGES
of America

THE
WHITE MOUNTAINS

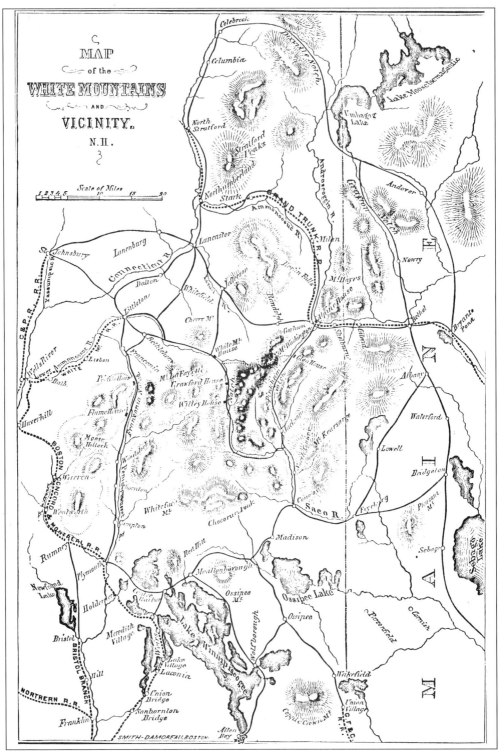

A map of the White Mountains and vicinity from the 1866 edition of Thomas Starr King's *The White Hills: Their Legends, Landscape, and Poetry.*

IMAGES
of America

THE
WHITE MOUNTAINS

Compiled by
Randall H. Bennett

ARCADIA

First published 1994
Reprinted 1995
Copyright © Randall H. Bennett, 1994

ISBN 0 7524 0077 0

Published by Arcadia Publishing,
an imprint of the Chalford Publishing Corporation,
One Washington Center, Dover, New Hampshire 03820.
Printed in Great Britain

OTHER PUBLICATIONS BY RANDALL H. BENNETT

As Author:
Oxford County, Maine: A Guide to Its Historic Architecture (1987)
A Fifield Genealogy: Some Descendants of William Fifield (1989)
Bethel, Maine: An Illustrated History (1991)

As Editor:
Sketches of Oxford County (1830; 1975)
The History of Rumford, Maine (1975)
Sunday River Sketches: A New England Chronicle (1977)
The History of Bethel, Maine (1994)

Contents

To the memory of my father, Lester L. Bennett,
and in honor of my mother, Bessie M. Bennett.

Introduction

The White Mountain region, with its lofty, granite-capped peaks, steep-sided notches, and sweeping valleys, long ago captured the public's imagination. These "Cristall Hills" (as they were called in the 1620s) are unique for their combination of superb scenery, important historical associations, and easy accessibility to millions of people in the northeastern part of the United States. A segment of the Appalachian chain that runs through northern New Hampshire and northwestern Maine some 70 miles inland from the Atlantic, the White Mountains may have been known to European explorers as early as the 1520s, when "high mountains" were sighted off the New England coast by Giovanni da Verrazano. A little more than a century later, Darby Field's pioneering 1642 ascent of Mount Washington initiated a period of discovery that is still taking place today. Indians, farmers, scientists, artists, innkeepers, tourists, loggers, and conservationists have all figured prominently in the story of these fabled mountains. Hundreds of books, beginning with Lucy Crawford's *The History of the White Mountains from the First Settlement of Upper Coos and Pequaket*, published in 1846, have appeared over the years documenting this relatively small geographic area. So extensive has this literature been that one bibliographer stated in 1911 that "the White Mountains . . . have had more written about them, probably, than any other mountains, the Alps alone excepted."

Based on an extensive private collection of White Mountain images, many of which have never been published before, this book aims to present a chronological record of some of the people, localities, and events that have given these ancient hills their extraordinary character. The task of selecting illustrations for inclusion in this volume was made more difficult with the realization that to include photographs of every White Mountain locale or event of significance would have filled many volumes, and thus, the photographs and engravings reproduced herein are meant to provide a representative rather than comprehensive overview of the region's history. Because historical events do not occur in isolation, organizing the text and images in a chronological rather than topical or geographic arrangement seemed the best way to treat such a broad subject.

Once known as the "Switzerland of America," the White Mountain region of Maine and New Hampshire has been strongly influenced over the last two centuries by tourism and outdoor recreation. As a result, a large number of the images in this volume deal in some way with this interesting and important aspect of the area's past. During the 1780s, a number of individuals visited the White Mountains initially to make scientific observations, but these scientists, like the writers, poets, and painters who soon followed them, were as much taken with the region's scenic grandeur as they were with its unusual plant and animal life. Their reports, many of which were published in leading journals of the day, encouraged other "tourists" to visit the area. Dating back to 1803, when a "house of entertainment" was built by Captain Eleazar Rosebrook near Bretton Woods in the town of Carroll, NH, the summer hotel industry in the White Mountains grew rapidly, especially during the first half of the nineteenth century when there was an ever-increasing demand by the public for accommodations that were both comfortable and convenient. By the early 1850s railroads had begun to push their way through the mountains, bringing countless numbers of tourists to even larger hotels that soon boasted, among other things, gas lighting, European-style cuisine, and their own post offices. All but a memory today, these grand hotels appear once again within the pages of this book in photographs that were often sold as postcards and mailed home to friends and relatives from the hotels themselves. Known throughout the world for its extreme weather conditions, Mount Washington, which at 6,288 feet is the Northeast's highest summit, long ago became the central focus of White Mountain tourism, and numerous photographs on and around the mountain are also included in these pages.

Most of the White Mountain views contained in this volume are part of a collection built up by the compiler over a twenty-five-year period, but a number of photographs have also been generously loaned by other collectors and organizations in the White Mountain region. For their courtesy in allowing publication of certain photographs, I would like to extend my sincere appreciation to Allan Fraser, Rudolph Honkala, Stanley Howe, Diane Jones, and the Bethel and Fryeburg, Maine, Historical Societies. For clarifying certain matters regarding the careers of White Mountain photographers Guy Shorey and Winston Pote, my thanks go to Guy Gosselin, Executive Director of the Mount Washington Observatory.

Randall H. Bennett

One

The White Mountains
are "Discovered"

AERIAL PHOTO, MT. WASHINGTON AND NORTHERN PEAKS, WHITE MTS, N.H.

Some of the most venerable mountains in the world, the White Mountains of Maine and New Hampshire achieved their present appearance soon after the end of the last Ice Age, although weathering and erosion continue to shape the region. The peaks of the Presidential Range were once covered with a layer of ice a mile thick, and large scratches in the granite testify to the awesome power of these ancient ice flows.

With Mount Washington in the far distance, this view of Carrigain Notch and the sheer cliffs of Mount Lowell is one of the finest in the White Mountains. Part of the "Pemigewasset Wilderness," the area is notable for its pristine state.

Glacial "erratics," such as the huge Madison Boulder at Madison, NH, were left behind as a massive ice sheet retreated from the White Mountain region some ten thousand years ago. The area's distinctive U-shaped valleys (called notches) and rounded mountain tops were also created by glacial action.

The Basin at Franconia Notch is a glacial pothole 30 feet in diameter and 15 feet deep. Sands and small stones carried by the swirling waters of the Pemigewasset River have smoothed the granite, creating this remarkable natural formation.

The White Horse and Cathedral Ledges tower above the winding Saco River to the west of North Conway village. Often painted by nineteenth century landscape artists, these spectacular granite outcroppings are now a haven for technical rock and ice climbers.

The Mysterious Hanging Boulder, Polar Caves
Near Plymouth, N. H.

An early postcard view of Polar Caves at Rumney, NH, in the southern White Mountains. Formed by frost activity over thousands of years, this extensive slab cave system has long been a major tourist attraction in the region.

MT. WASHINGTON

The high summits of the White Mountains were seen by mariners off the northern New England coast as early as the 1520s. The term itself, first seen in print in 1672, may originate from the fact that, under certain atmospheric conditions, the mica schist atop many of these mountains gives them a white or whitish-gray aspect when seen from a distance, even in summer.

12

Among the most interesting physical features of the White Mountains are the treeless high elevations found in the Presidential and Franconia Ranges. In these so-called "alpine zones" (above 4800 feet) are found rare flowers and other vegetation whose growth has been stunted by the harsh climate. In this photo, the AMC's Greenleaf Hut, with Cannon Mountain and Echo Lake beyond, lies below the rough open slopes of Mount Lafayette.

The fertile valleys surrounding these mountains were once inhabited by Abenaki Indians with such familiar names as Passaconaway, Kancamagus, and Chocorua, but because few written records were made during their lifetimes, such individuals today are more the stuff of legend than fact. This view of Chocorua Lake and Mountain is one of the most photographed in the region.

THE INDIAN HEAD, WHITE MOUNTAINS OF N.H.

Located atop 2,554-foot Mount Pemigewasset, the Indian Head profile at Franconia Notch is a fascinating and permanent reminder of the long Abenaki presence in the White Mountains previous to the arrival of Europeans.

In June 1642, Darby Field of Exeter, NH, became the first caucasian to ascend Mount Washington. His account of this trip mentions the thick cloud cover and two ponds (Lakes of the Clouds) encountered on the way to the summit, once thought by local Indians to be the abode of the Great Spirit. Field's glowing report of mineral riches discovered on this peak fired other daring men to undertake the exploration of the White Mountains.

A monument erected in 1904 at Fryeburg, ME, marks the spot where, on May 8, 1725, some forty members of the Pigwacket Indians were killed by a group of Massachusetts Rangers under the command of Captain John Lovewell. This skirmish, in which the Indian leader Paugus was also killed, so alarmed the area's native inhabitants that most moved north to the relative safety of the St. Francis Mission in Canada.

Fryeburg, ME, and Conway, NH, were the first communities in the central White Mountain area to be permanently settled by caucasians in the 1760s. Village centers and prosperous farms soon appeared throughout the region, although agriculture was less successful in the higher elevations. Most of the early settlers' homes, such as this example at Randolph, NH, were modestly constructed.

Timothy Nash discovered the "Gate of the Notch," at the north end of Crawford Notch, while on a hunting expedition on nearby Cherry Mountain in 1771. By 1774 a primitive road had been constructed that provided an important link between the upper Connecticut valley and the seacoast. An improved road, the Tenth New Hampshire Turnpike, was built in 1807.

In 1784 a group of Massachusetts and New Hampshire men, including the historian Jeremy Belknap, ventured up Mount Washington to make scientific observations. Due to rainy weather and heavy cloud cover, an accurate measurement of the summit's altitude could not be taken, but unusual plant specimens and the local topography were duly noted.

Two

Pioneers
and Early Visitors

Built c. 1799, the Peabody Tavern at Gilead, ME, is a significant White Mountain landmark that dates back to the beginnings of tourism in this region. Listed in the *National Register of Historic Places*, the Peabody Tavern once provided rustic lodgings on the stage route from Lancaster, NH, to Portland, ME.

A view of Franconia Notch and the Pemigewasset River from the south. On the left are the precipitous granite ledges of Cannon Mountain and, at right, the towering summit of Mount Lafayette, at 5,249 feet the highest peak in the Franconia Range. Such dramatic scenery must have challenged those who built the first road through Franconia Notch in the first decade of the nineteenth century.

The Franconia Ridge, with its landslide-scarred peaks, extends from Mount Flume in the south to Mount Lafayette in the north. The earliest published accounts of mountain climbing in this area date from the 1820s, well before the Ridge Trail, on the right in this photo, was created. Over a million people a year now hike or visit the natural and man-made features in the Franconia Notch area.

Made famous in the mid-nineteenth century by Nathaniel Hawthorne's 1848 short story, "The Great Stone Face," the Old Man of the Mountain was discovered sometime around 1805 by Luke Brooks, then tax collector for the town of Franconia. Part of a team of men surveying land along the Notch road, Brooks was supposedly filling a pail with water from Profile Lake when, looking up, he was startled by what appeared to be the likeness of a man's face in the granite cliffs. Even more amazing was the fact that these human-like features were in perfect focus only within a limited area near the lake. Later investigations revealed that this remarkable natural formation, suspended 1200 feet above Profile Lake and 3200 feet above sea level, extended some 40 feet from forehead to chin and 25 feet in width. So unusual is this rock profile that, over the years, millions of people from all over the world have traveled to Franconia Notch to see the gigantic silhouette for themselves.

One of the earliest tourist attractions in the White Mountains, the Flume is a natural granite gorge nearly 800 feet long with walls between 12 and 20 feet apart and 70 to 90 feet high. The Flume was supposedly discovered in 1808 by "Aunt Jess" Guernsey, a ninety-three-year-old woman who came upon the great stone canyon while fishing at the base of Mount Liberty. Amid lush vegetation and the rushing waters of Flume Brook, nineteenth-century visitors to the Flume marvelled as they wandered along a primitive boardwalk and under the famous "suspended boulder," which was dislodged in a storm-caused avalanche in 1883. Today, this dramatic gorge, once filled with molten lava, continues to fascinate thousands of visitors annually.

Known as the "Patriarch of the Mountains," Abel Crawford was a pioneering pathbuilder, mountain guide, and innkeeper who settled in Hart's Location, below the southern end of what is now Crawford Notch, some time before 1820. At the age of seventy-four, Crawford was the first to ascend Mount Washington on horseback.

Built by Abel Crawford and his son Ethan Allen Crawford in 1819, the 8-mile-long Crawford Path, in the center of this photo, has been called the nation's oldest continuously maintained recreation trail. The oldest section, built from the Crawford House site to Mount Clinton, was originally a footpath that was later extended to the summit of Mount Washington. In 1840 Thomas J. Crawford, Abel's younger son, converted the trail into a bridle-path.

21

Of the events that helped focus national attention on the White Mountains before the Civil War, the famous "Willey Disaster" stands out as by far the most significant. On the fateful night of August 28, 1826, the family of Samuel Willey, Jr., including his wife, five children, a hired man, and a boy, were alarmed by the roar of an avalanche descending on their modest home deep in the confines of Crawford Notch. Fleeing to a nearby shelter that was assumed to be a safe haven, the family instead ran directly into the path of a thundering mass of trees and rocks and were all killed; three of the bodies were never recovered from the devastation on the valley floor. Beyond the tragedy of these deaths, the element in this incident that captured the public's imagination and led to the establishment of the Willey House as an American cultural icon, was the sparing of the residence when the landslide divided in two, passing by on either side. This photograph of the Willey House was taken c. 1880.

Soon after the Willey Disaster, hundreds of tourists began to flock to the scene of this great catastrophe. To accommodate these visitors, Horace Fabyan of Portland, ME, built a hotel next to the Willey House in 1845 (both buildings burned in September 1899). Mount Willard's precipitous cliffs rise in the background of this early stereograph view taken by the Kilburn Brothers studio of Littleton, NH.

Made famous by the tragedy of 1826, these boulders divided the landslide that spared the Willey House but killed its occupants.

A view of Crawford Notch, looking south from the top of Mount Willard. The site of the Willey Disaster is at center, with Mount Webster on the left and Mount Willey (the source of the destructive landslide) on the right.

The Notch House, at the northern entrance to Crawford Notch, opened in 1829 under Thomas J. Crawford's management as the first structure in the mountains built specifically to house tourists. To amuse their guests, the Crawfords captured live deer, bears, wolves, and moose, and fired a cannon near the Notch House to produce resounding echoes. This is an engraving after a drawing by William H. Bartlett, a London illustrator whose work appeared in the book *American Scenery*, published in 1838/9.

The Bemis House-Bemis-White Mountains N H

The Bemis House at "Notchland," near the southern end of Crawford Notch, was constructed for Dr. Samuel Bemis, a successful Boston dentist who resided here from 1840 to 1881. Bemis took some of the earliest landscape photographs in this country in the vicinity of his granite-walled home. Abel Crawford's "Mount Crawford House" once stood directly across the road from this structure, which is now operated as an inn.

The former home of Hayes and Dolly Copp gained local prominence in the early nineteenth century as a place where weary travelers could get a meal and a night's lodging. It is now the site of a well-known White Mountain National Forest campground between Gorham, NH, and Pinkham Notch.

The White Mountain House north of Bretton Woods was begun sometime previous to 1843, and was operated for a time by the legendary "Giant of the Hills," Ethan Allen Crawford. Horace Fabyan, known in later years for his ownership and management of the nearby Fabyan House, completed the structure, as seen here, in 1848. This early hotel survived into the 1920s.

LITTLETON, N. H. Thayer House.

Boasting high Greek Revival columns and an eight-sided rooftop cupola, Thayer's Hotel in Littleton, NH, was begun in 1848 and probably ranks as the oldest hotel structure in the White Mountain region. In the nineteenth century the hotel was well-known for its fashionable accommodations and fine cuisine.

Three

The Golden Age
of Tourism

A coach-and-four descends from Pinkham Notch with Mount Washington looming in the background. Before the railroad's arrival in 1851, travel through the mountains was by foot, horse, or stage.

The construction of the Atlantic and St. Lawrence Railroad through the northern part of the White Mountains brought great economic benefits to the region as a whole. Connecting Portland, ME, with Montreal, PQ, the railway line arrived at Gorham, NH, in 1851, where a combination station and hotel called the Alpine House was built that year. In this photograph a train prepares to depart from the station at nearby Bethel, ME.

The coming of the railroad and Gorham's vantage point just a few miles north of Mount Washington combined to make this New Hampshire town a major tourist destination, beginning in the 1850s. The second Alpine House is at center; built in 1876, it was later moved back and connected to the smaller Mount Madison House hotel.

The first Glen House, begun in 1852, became a highly successful enterprise under the management of Joseph M. Thompson in the 1850s and '60s. Before his untimely death by drowning in the nearby Peabody River in 1869, "Landlord" Thompson helped to popularize the Pinkham Notch area as a summer retreat by building paths to many nearby waterfalls and other points of interest, including Mount Washington, in whose shadow Thompson's hotel stood. Commanding one of the grandest views in the White Mountains, the Glen House was eventually doubled in size under the ownership of brothers Charles R. and Weston F. Milliken. Business prospered throughout the 1870s and early 1880s, but as the hotel was being closed in October 1884, a fire in one wing was discovered, and soon the famous old hostelry was a smouldering pile of ashes. Within a year's time, the proprietors had rebuilt on the same site, choosing Portland architect Francis H. Fassett's "English Cottage" design for a hotel that stood nearly 300 feet long and three-and-a-half stories high. The second Glen House also had a veranda about 450 feet long, and accommodations for five hundred guests. Like its predecessor, however, this hotel was also built entirely of wood, and a fire from an unknown cause leveled the grand structure on Sunday evening, July 16, 1893. So great was this loss to the owners that another large hotel was not built. However, the former staff dormitory, also called "Glen House," was utilized from 1901 to 1924 to house a limited number of visitors.

The 100-by-60-foot parlor or "drawing room" of the first Glen House, with its elegant furnishings, ornate chandeliers, and stylish carpet, was the largest in any American hotel at the time of its completion in the 1850s.

Well-to-do guests who ate in the dining hall of the first Glen House enjoyed bountiful, full-course meals comparable to those in fine city hotels. Strips of floorcloth sewn together and elegant plaster ceiling medallions are just two of the many interesting features revealed in this Kilburn Brothers stereograph view from the 1870s.

The Garnet Pool, "a wild and sequestered nook," could be reached by a short walk from the Glen House. White Mountain hotel-keepers of the mid-nineteenth century attracted visitors by offering a variety of short excursions like this one. Croquet, golf, tennis, horseback riding, and mountain climbing were also popular activities in and around the hotels.

Some 70 feet high and located a short distance off the highway in Pinkham Notch, the Glen Ellis Falls received its name in 1852. It had previously been called the "Pitcher Falls" because of the way in which water poured over the top.

31

The first Summit House on Mount Washington was opened in July 1852 in response to the increasing number of tourists coming up the mountain. Stone was blasted for its walls and lumber was brought up on pack horses. The heavy front door was carried up the mountain from the Glen House by Lucius Rosebrook of Lancaster, who, legend has it, also carried a jug of molasses in his hand "for good measure." To prevent damage from high winds, the building was bound down by 2-inch cables which were cemented into the rocks.

Dinners at the first Summit House cost $1, and $2.50 was charged for three meals and a night's lodging. On August 23, 1853, Jefferson Davis, then secretary of war in Franklin Pierce's cabinet and later to become president of the Southern Confederacy, stayed the night in this rude shelter, which remained in use until 1884.

The Tip Top House, constructed in 1853 and opened late in July of that year, is the oldest structure remaining on the summit of Mount Washington. Like the first Summit House, Tip Top has walls of granite that are several feet thick, enabling it to withstand even the fiercest winter storms. Its recently restored flat deck roof, seen here in a photograph from the early 1860s, allowed visitors an unobstructed view of the surrounding countryside that was aided on cloudless days by a telescope. One visitor, recalling a visit to the newly-opened Tip Top House in 1853, remarked, "Just beside the outside door stood the affable bartender, backed by various decanters, from which he dispensed at once to all new comers the health-giving elixir that was considered more necessary than food even. The house was finished inside, and partitioned with cotton cloth. The bedsteads were berths above each other, as in a steamer, made of fir poles brought up on horseback. The beds were filled with moss."

Franconia Notch was fast becoming a fashionable playground for the urban elite when the first Profile House, a 110-room grand hotel, opened on July 3, 1853. Accommodating from four hundred to five hundred guests in its original form, the Profile House was enlarged in 1865 and again in 1872. A number of tastefully designed summer cottages connected with boardwalks were eventually built adjacent to the hotel to house visitors who desired more privacy. By the end of the nineteenth century, the Profile House offered guests such improvements as gas lamps, a barber shop, private baths, bowling alleys, a railway station served by a narrow-gauge railroad, and fireworks displays over Echo Lake. The building on the right, sporting a long row of roof dormers, was originally the Lafayette House, which opened in 1835 as the first hotel in Franconia Notch. It was moved by the Profile House owners from a spot 100 yards north of the present Lafayette Place Campground and used as a servants' quarters. Most everything in this c. 1880 photograph was torn down in the fall of 1905 to make way for the second Profile House.

Franconia Notch, Echo Lake, and the first Profile House hotel from the scenic overlook known as "Artist Bluff." The beauty of Franconia Notch has encouraged visits by many notable Americans over the years. Among those who have come to this spectacular mountain pass for rest and relaxation have been writers Nathaniel Hawthorne, John Greenleaf Whittier, William Cullen Bryant, Henry Wadsworth Longfellow, Edward Everett Hale, Ralph Waldo Emerson, and James Russell Lowell, artists Thomas Cole, Albert Bierstadt, Edward Hill, Asher Brown Durand, and John Frederick Kensett, religious leaders Henry Ward Beecher and Mary Baker Eddy, and former Presidents Andrew Jackson, Franklin Pierce, Ulysses S. Grant, Grover Cleveland, Calvin Coolidge, and Dwight D. Eisenhower.

Ida, a small steamboat owned by the Profile House, once plied the waters of Echo Lake. The granite ledges of Eagle Cliff rise in the background.

The headwaters of the Pemigewasset River, Profile Lake was once known as "Ferrin's Pond," the "Old Man's Mirror," and the "Old Man's Washbowl." This 15-acre lake is now a haven for fly fishermen.

Long dresses and relatively formal attire were in vogue late in the nineteenth century when these tourists visited the Cascade, near the Basin in Franconia Notch.

Posing for the stereograph photographer near the top of 25-foot Avalanche Falls, this group of people (the same as in the photo above) has just emerged from the cool recesses of the Flume.

37

The Mount Washington Road Company was chartered in 1853, and construction of the Carriage Road (now the "Auto Road") commenced the following summer. Originated by General David O. Macomber of Middletown, CT, the plan called for special horse-drawn "omnibuses" that could be leveled and that would carry passengers to and from a massive stone summit house with an observatory.

Utilizing horses, oxen, and large quantities of black powder, laborers completed 2 miles of the Mount Washington Carriage Road in the first year of work. In this very early Bierstadt Brothers photograph of the lower portion of the road, the Toll House stands at center, with piles of wood, from trees cut as the construction progressed, stacked neatly across the road.

Four miles of the Carriage Road had been built by the end of 1856, when the Road Company went bankrupt due to high construction costs. Built in 1855 to shelter workers, the historic Halfway House burned on December 6, 1984. Note the mountain wagon and weathered "scrub" in this stereograph photo.

A lone wagon and driver approach The Horn, a short distance above the Halfway House at the 4,000-foot mark on the Carriage Road. From here on, the road is above treeline.

Two men admire the view from just below The Horn. On the right a low wall of stone separates the Carriage Road from the chasm known as the Great Gulf.

A reorganized "Mount Washington Summit Road Company" was formed in 1859, and work began again the next year to push the Carriage Road to the summit (see page 50). Taken from a section of the Carriage Road known as "Five Mile Grade," this Guy Shorey photograph provides an interesting contrast between the massive northern Presidentials and the tiny Halfway House on Mount Washington's eastern flank.

First discovered by Ethan Allen Crawford, the Snow Arch in Tuckerman Ravine is an interesting feature that is sometimes formed when brooks descending over the headwall eat away at the huge piles of snow at its base. On July 16, 1854, while on a survey of the Carriage Road, three men dined in the Snow Arch. It was then 260 feet long, 84 feet wide, and 40 feet high to the roof. While they ate, icy cold water constantly dripped down, and a heavy thundershower passed over them.

The awe-inspiring beauty of the Snow Arch belies its danger. In 1886 fifteen-year-old Sewall Faunce was killed when part of the Arch fell, and eight years later a party of Appalachian Mountain Club members narrowly missed being crushed by a 100-foot section.

Lost River Gorge is a remarkable series of glacial caverns 40 to 75 feet deep that extend for about half a mile through Kinsman Notch. Located 6 miles west of North Woodstock, these fascinating caves were first explored in the 1850s by Royal and Lyman Jackman. Regular guided tours began in 1893, but earlier visits by tourists are on record.

In 1912 the Society for the Protection of New Hampshire Forests acquired 148 acres surrounding and including the Lost River Gorge, thereby protecting it for the enjoyment of future generations. Soon after this acquisition, improvements were made in the form of wooden walkways, ladders, and bridges throughout the gorge. The Rollins Shelter, dating also from this period, now serves as a gift shop.

During the "Golden Age" of tourism in the White Mountains, visitors wishing to scale Mount Lafayette, once known as the "Great Haystack," used a bridle path that originated near the Lafayette House hotel in Franconia Notch. Somewhat resembling the first Summit House on Mount Washington to the east, the Mount Lafayette shelter was built partly of stone to withstand the harsh elements above treeline. Despite its substantial construction, the building seems to have fallen into disuse soon after the Civil War and had "disappeared" by 1875. Notwithstanding, remnants of this early mountaintop refuge, depicted in the *c.* 1858 photograph above, may still be observed by modern-day hikers.

From 1853 until about 1887, "Professor" John Merrill became renowned as the "Man at the Pool," spending each summer at Franconia Notch rowing visitors around and entertaining them with his unique brand of homespun philosophy. The Sentinel Pine Bridge, built atop a 175-foot tree toppled during the 1938 hurricane, now spans the falls above this large glacial formation.

Jackson's first and only hotel for many years, the Jackson Falls House was opened to the public in 1858. In 1885 the building was raised and a new first story, with high-ceilinged rooms, was built beneath it. This landmark closed by the 1970s and is no longer standing.

The rising popularity of the Crawford Notch area resulted in the construction, in 1852, of the first Crawford House hotel on a knoll west of Saco Lake. When that structure burned on April 30, 1859, steps were immediately taken to erect a replacement, and within sixty days another hotel, on an even larger scale, stood on the same site, despite the fact that the lumber had to be hauled 17 miles! To celebrate this accomplishment, one hundred guests were served an elegant meal in the dining room on the Fourth of July. Beginning in 1870, the Crawford House and several other nearby hotels came under the successful management of the Barron, Merrill, & Barron Co., founded by Asa Barron of White River Junction, VT. Asa's son, "Colonel" William Barron, carried on the family hotel-keeping tradition at the Crawford House until 1947. This famous view of the second Crawford House is from the top of "Elephant's Head," a granite outcropping above the Gate of the Notch.

This stereograph from the studio of N.W. Pease of North Conway is entitled, "Starting for Mt. Washington, from Crawford House, NH." The use of saddle ponies to ascend trails like the Crawford Path declined with the opening of the Carriage Road and Cog Railway in the 1860s.

The second Crawford House was especially noted for the wide span of its dining room and ballroom ceilings, as well as its elevator operated by water power. The hotel's parlor, seen here, offered comfortable furnishings and gas lights.

Boating on Saco Lake, near the Crawford House, was a relaxing pastime for tourists who, before the advent of the automobile, came to the White Mountains "for the season."

A dozen Rocky Mountain burros owned by the Crawford House once carried guests on day trips that were advertised as "novel, safe, and enjoyable" in the hotel literature. Some of the more popular destinations were Mounts Washington, Avalon, Clinton, and Willard, the latter of which provided this panorama of Crawford Notch. Such merriment was at one time called "burromobiling."

"English Jack," also known as the "Crawford Notch Hermit," was a picturesque White Mountain character who built his shanty just above the Gate of the Notch in the late 1870s. Jack's entertaining stories and rather unorthodox eating habits (he once ate half of an uncooked striped snake "with apparent relish") earned him a special place with tourists traveling through Crawford Notch. He died in 1912.

Reverend Thomas Starr King authored the classic 1859 work *The White Hills: Their Legends, Landscape, and Poetry*. His name is preserved today by Mount Starr King in Jefferson and by King Ravine, a tremendous gorge on the north side of Mount Adams.

Beginning in the 1820s and lasting to the present day, artists have sought inspiration from the "sublime" scenery of the White Mountains. In the late 1840s, the famous "White Mountain School" blossomed in the North Conway area under artist Benjamin Champney, the first painter to reside year-round in the mountains. Depicting the northern Presidential Range from the Androscoggin River at Bethel, ME, this pastoral landscape is a typical late-nineteenth century example.

Called the "North Conway of the eastern slope" by White Mountain enthusiast and author Reverend Thomas Starr King, Bethel, ME, boasted several good hotels by the mid-1860s. The Bethel House, at the south end of the village common, was constructed in 1861 and remained a highly popular destination for many years.

Amid much fanfare, the Mount Washington Carriage Road was officially opened to the summit on August 8, 1861. Three weeks before the event, Joseph M. Thompson, proprietor of the Glen House, was the first to reach the top in this wagon, though assistance was needed to keep it upright over the uncompleted last stretch of road.

North Conway's Kearsarge House was begun in 1861 and greatly enlarged over the years. In 1863, Mary Todd Lincoln, with her sons Robert and Thomas, spent two days at the hotel before venturing on to the Glen House and the summit of Mount Washington.

Soon after the completion of the Carriage Road, the Tip Top House was enlarged by adding a second story with seventeen little bedrooms. After the second Summit House was opened in 1873, Tip Top was used for several years by hotel and railway employees. Note the pack horse and substantial pile of wood.

The Twin Mountain House, constructed in 1868 several miles north of Bretton Woods, was a favorite retreat of Reverend Henry Ward Beecher and his sister, Harriet Beecher Stowe, for some seventeen years beginning in 1872. His fiery Sunday sermons, held in a tent set up next to the hotel, were long remembered by the large crowds who attended.

In 1867, Dexter Blodgett built two wire bridges over the Androscoggin River at Gorham, NH, and developed a resort beneath an impressive waterfall that he called the Alpine Cascades. Twenty-five cents was charged to cross the river and gain admission to Blodgett's popular attraction.

A primitive merry-go-round at the foot of the Alpine Cascades at Gorham provided an added amusement for visitors. Note the elaborate staircase to the right of the waterfall.

The brainchild of inventor Sylvester Marsh, the Mount Washington Cog Railway easily became the premier White Mountain tourist attraction at its opening in 1869. Marsh had made his fortune in the meat packing business in Ohio and, after experiencing a difficult climb to Mount Washington's summit in 1857, became determined to design a safer and easier way to the top. Awarded a patent for an "improved" cogwheel locomotive by 1865, Marsh soon received a charter from the New Hampshire Legislature to construct his "Railway to the Moon." The first engine, named "Hero" but soon afterwards dubbed "Peppersass," successfully climbed a section of test tract amid the stares of railroad officials, stockholders, and other invited guests on August 29, 1866. Under the newly organized Mount Washington Steam Railway Company, work proceeded rapidly over the next three years, with the first train arriving on the summit on July 3, 1869. (Europe's first cog railway, on Mount Rigi in Switzerland, was patterned after that on Mount Washington and opened in 1871.) Mount Washington passengers then, as now, frequently held their breath as they slowly ascended "Jacob's Ladder," a 300-foot trestle that reaches an incredible 37.41 percent grade!

Guests at the Crawford House and other nearby hotels were transported to the "Marshfield" base station of the Cog Railway by Concord stagecoaches at the time of this *c.* 1875 stereograph.

The earliest engines on the Cog Railway featured vertical boilers, but by 1878 more powerful locomotives with horizontal boilers had appeared. Today's engines, traveling at 4 miles per hour, consume a ton of coal and over 1000 gallons of water on each trip up the mountain.

Slideboards, or "Devil's Shingles," allowed workmen to rapidly descend Mount Washington (sometimes at an average speed of 60 miles per hour!) at the end of the day. About 1930, after a number of serious accidents occurred, these picturesque but hazardous 1-by-3-foot planks with primitive brakes were banned.

As a way of further dramatizing the steepness of Jacob's Ladder, nineteenth-century stereo view photographers were not averse to tilting their cameras. Such views no doubt enticed many tourists to experience the extraordinary ride for themselves.

During an earlier era, winter ascents of Mount Washington via the snow and ice-covered Cog Railway track were not unknown.

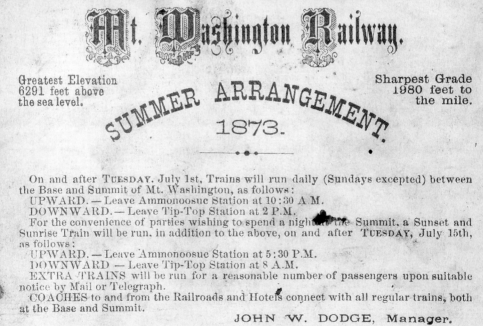

Mt. Washington Railway.

Greatest Elevation
6291 feet above
the sea level.

SUMMER ARRANGEMENT.
1873.

Sharpest Grade
1980 feet to
the mile.

On and after TUESDAY. July 1st, Trains will run daily (Sundays excepted) between the Base and Summit of Mt. Washington, as follows:
UPWARD. — Leave Ammonoosuc Station at 10 : 30 A M.
DOWNWARD. — Leave Tip-Top Station at 2 P.M.
For the convenience of parties wishing to spend a night the Summit, a Sunset and Sunrise Train will be run, in addition to the above, on and after TUESDAY, July 15th, as follows:
UPWARD. — Leave Ammonoosuc Station at 5 : 30 P.M.
DOWNWARD — Leave Tip-Top Station at 8 A.M.
EXTRA TRAINS will be run for a reasonable number of passengers upon suitable notice by Mail or Telegraph.
COACHES to and from the Railroads and Hotels connect with all regular trains, both at the Base and Summit.

JOHN W. DODGE, Manager.

This seasonal timetable for 1873 was issued during the last year the Cog Railway operated entirely with vertical-boiler locomotives.

An 1880 photograph of the Cog Railway climbing the summit cone provides a close-up look at the central cog rail that allowed trains to safely ascend and descend Mount Washington. On the right are the second Summit House, built in 1872 (see page 59), the roof of the first Summit House, and, next to the track, the famous Lizzie Bourne Monument, which reads, "Lizzie Bourne, Daughter of Judge Bourne, Kennebunk, Me., Perished Here Sept. 14, 1855, Aged 20 Yrs." One of over a hundred people who have died on Mount Washington, Miss Bourne was in the company of her uncle and his daughter late that September day when bad weather and darkness overcame them. Unable to find the summit buildings, they lay down to spend the night, and Lizzie died soon afterwards from exhaustion and a slight heart defect. Accounts of this death, the second on the mountain, appeared in many papers and captivated a curious public.

Built in 1870 and refurbished in 1965, the Paddleford truss covered bridge at Jackson, NH, is one of a handful of similar spans to have survived in the White Mountains.

The U.S. Signal Service established the first permanent weather station atop Mount Washington in November 1870. Four years later, this heavily braced structure was erected on the summit to house observers. Year-round recordings were made from this building through the winter of 1886/7, and each summer until 1892.

Constructed in 1872-73 by the Cog Railway under Walter Aiken's supervision, the second Mount Washington Summit House was the largest hotel in this country on any mountain of such height when it opened in July of 1873. Some 250 freight trains were required to bring up the lumber for the two-and-a-half story structure, which boasted nearly one hundred "sleeping rooms" and its own orchestra. So securely was the building bolted to the rocks and cabled down, that it later withstood winds recorded at over 186 miles per hour with little or no damage. The cost of the hotel, exclusive of the freight charges (estimated at $10,000) was $56,599.57, a sizable sum in that period. It was not long, however, before capacity crowds had more than eliminated this debt, and the hotel had become the hub of a thriving summit community. The photograph above was likely taken during late spring, before all of the protective window shutters had been removed.

White Mountain historian Frederick W. Kilbourne, in his 1916 work, *Chronicles of the White Mountains*, said of the second Summit House, "Its cheerful office, with its great stove, was a welcome place to many a traveler arriving by railway, by carriage road, or by trail. Many a day weather conditions were such that visitors were marooned in the office during their entire stay on the Summit and were devoutly grateful for the hotel's hospitable shelter. Almost every evening of the season found a group of travelers whiling away the time enjoying the genial warmth of the stove and exchanging experiences of their mountain trips."

The large dining room in the second Summit House atop Mount Washington could seat up to 150 people at a time.

With several trains on the mountain, the Summit House platform could be a busy place on a summer afternoon. The dog on the right, "Medford," was once the summit's "official receptionist." Some of the more notable guests who visited the hotel over the years included President and Mrs. Rutherford Hayes, P.T. Barnum (who, tradition has it, called the view from the top "The Second Greatest Show on Earth!"), General George McClellan, and Admiral Robert E. Peary.

Three Carriage Road Company mountain wagons, an early vertical-boiler Cog Railway engine and car, and the huge second Summit House stand out against Mount Washington's rock-strewn summit in this stereograph view.

The second Flume House was located only a short distance from such natural attractions as the Flume and the Pool. Built in 1872 and destroyed by fire in 1918, this gambrel-roofed hotel had a season that normally ran from June 1 to October 15. As a way of enticing guests, the back of this turn-of-the-century advertising card included the following message: "The Flume House has recently been enlarged and refitted, and has accommodations for one hundred guests. It is heated by open fireplaces and a furnace, and furnished with electric bells and other modern appliances, including telephone communication with all the towns within a radius of 20 miles and a quick telegraph connection via the Profile House."

The White Mountain Club of Portland became the second organization of climbers in North America when it gathered in 1873. Though it lasted only a little over a decade, this pioneering group of hikers blazed a number of new trails in the Mahoosuc Range of mountains in western Maine. These turn-of-the-century hikers are on Mount Washington's Gulfside Trail.

The dark pools and sparkling waterfalls at the Albany Basins, located a short distance east of the Maine/New Hampshire border, drew crowds of summer tourists in the post-Civil War era. A small hotel stood for a brief time at the entrance to these cascades.

One of the more interesting legends connected with the White Mountains involves the "Giant's Grave," a substantial mound of river gravel at Bretton Woods on which stood two early hotels that burned in succession. According to tradition, an Indian, waving a burning pitchpine torch kindled at a tree struck by lightning, cried out the prophecy, "No paleface shall take deep root here; this the Great Spirit whispered in my ear." Despite the supposed warning, and a number of spring freshets that did considerable damage at this location, the mound was leveled in 1872 and the imposing hotel above constructed on the site. The Fabyan House, named in honor of the well-known innkeeper Horace Fabyan, opened to guests in 1873, and soon became a favorite with America's rich and famous. Centrally located at the junction of several rail lines, this elegant hotel existed much longer than its predecessors, though fire claimed the building in 1951.

The grand hotels of the White Mountains annually hired hundreds of people to serve as waitresses, porters, chambermaids, bellmen, caddies, and cooks. In the 1870s this group of men and women provided hospitality at the Fabyan House.

For many years the Fabyan House parlor was the scene of well-attended evening entertainments. Lecturers, choral groups, magicians, actors, and religious leaders traveled throughout the mountains visiting many of the hotels.

The construction of the Portland and Ogdensburg Railroad through Crawford Notch in the early 1870s was an engineering feat many thought impossible. Primitive derricks were used to remove blasted rock near the Gate of the Notch.

In order to create a place for the railroad tracks, P&O workers blasted away the ledges along the base of Mount Willard. Between Bemis and the Crawford House, the grade was 116 feet to the mile for 9 consecutive miles.

66

Removing rock from "The Great Cut" at the Gate of the Notch, these laborers pause below the towering backdrop of Mount Webster.

Huge pieces of granite, many weighing several tons, were removed and used for fill as P&O construction crews made their way along the steep slopes of Crawford Notch.

67

Portland and Ogdensburg trains began running to the Fabyan House in August 1875. Company superintendent Jonas Hamilton (on the right) posed next to the engine "Willey" in the Great Cut for this stereograph view.

Financial difficulties delayed construction of the Vermont section of the P&O, and it was not until July 23, 1877, that the first passenger train ran from Portland, ME, to Burlington, VT. Much of the early wooden trestlework on the line was later replaced with stone fill.

Often compared to the opening of the Mount Washington Cog Railway, the laying out of the Portland and Ogdensburg Railroad through Crawford Notch was an achievement that received tremendous publicity in the 1870s and 1880s. Suspended between a 90-foot gorge and the towering cliffs of Mount Willard, a passenger train with an open observation car has halted briefly atop the Willey Brook Bridge. This much-photographed location was later made famous by Harrison Bird Brown's painting, "The Heart of the Notch."

Rising 80 feet above the ground, the Frankenstein Trestle, named for White Mountain artist Godfrey Frankenstein, allowed tourists to experience the thrills of "sky railroading" as they traveled through Crawford Notch. The spindly ironwork was later replaced with heavier steel. The building of the Portland and Ogdensburg Railroad greatly stimulated travel to the White Mountains and resulted in the opening of many new hotels and boarding houses. Last used for freight operations in 1983, the line may soon reopen for scenic passenger excursions.

The Appalachian Mountain Club was organized in 1876. While under Joe Dodge's watchful eye, "Porky Gulch," site of the AMC's much-expanded North Country headquarters, became a popular starting place for hiking expeditions on and around Mount Washington. The open vehicle at right was owned by the AMC, as indicated by the lettering on its side.

The first and for many years the only newspaper printed regularly on a major mountaintop, *Among the Clouds* was founded in 1877 by Henry M. Burt of Springfield, MA. For eight summers the paper was printed in an office set up inside the old Tip Top House.

BURT'S
Among the Clouds.

PRINTED DAILY ON THE SUMMIT OF MOUNT WASHINGTON.

VOL. I.　　　MOUNT WASHINGTON, N. H., FRIDAY, JULY 20, 1877.　　　NO. 1.

WEST SIDE NEWS.

The Appalachian Mountain Club held a meeting at the Fabyan House on Tuesday, July twenty-fourth, at half past two. This is the fourth field meeting.

A Saratoga and White Mountain express has been put on this season. The trains are run between the two points via the Wells River and Montpelier railroad.

Henry Ward Beecher goes to the Twin Mountain House in August to remain till October. He writes to Mr. Barron: "We are beginning to think a sniff of mountain air would be refreshing."

John Habberton, author of Helen's Babies, is registered at Phillips' Bellevue House, in Bethlehem. He has been over to the Profile House and later in the season goes to the Twin Mountain House.

The view from the Oak Hill House in Littleton is extensive and beautiful. Mt. Washington and the entire White Mountain range are in full view. Mr. Farr, the proprietor, keeps an excellent house for summer guests.

The new Episcopal church at Bethlehem, was occupied for the first time on Sunday the 8th. It is a tasteful little structure and meets the wants of summer visitors, who contributed the necessary funds to build it.

The White Mountain House is one of the oldest established in the mountain region. Mr. Rounsevel takes pains to keep a good house, and has had liberal patronage during each season. It is a mile west of Fabyan's.

The pioneer White Mountain express over the Boston, Concord and Montreal railroad is doing a good business. Drawing-room cars are run the same as usual to Boston and New London. Passengers dine at Plymouth, where they always get a good dinner.

Mr. Leavitt's Mount Pleasant House, near the Fabyan House, has been open but a year or two, and, although moderate in charges, it has a good reputation. The Mount Washington railway can be seen from the base to the summit from this house.

Hitherto Bethlehem has had only a Methodist church. The Episcopalians having built a church edifice the Congregationalists are following in the same direction and are now building a fine structure on a new street, near the Sinclair House. It is expected that services will be held in it before the season closes.

Rev. Nelson Millard, wife and son, of Syracuse, N. Y., are stopping at the Sinclair House in Bethlehem. Mr. Millard is pastor of the First Presbyterian church in Syracuse and has gone to Bethlehem on account of an asthmatic difficulty, where he hopes to find relief. The Sinclair is an excellent place for those who need rest.

The Sinclair House, under the management of Durgin & Fox, at Bethlehem, has gained golden opinions from those who have passed its portals. It is an excellent house and in point of reputation stands as well as could be desired. It is a good place to make either a long or a short stop. Durgin's smiling face makes everybody happy.

The "Governor Ingersoll," in charge of N. M. Parker, conductor, was the first drawing-room car that came through from New York on the new White Mountain express line. It left New York July ninth, at five minutes past eight, a. m., Springfield at one p. m., and reached the Fabyan House a little after nine the same evening. The car was well filled when it left New York. Connecticut Valley people who come to the mountains will appreciate this new arrangement.

Many of the members of the American Institute of Instruction who attended the meetings of the association at Montpelier, have been visiting the White Mountains. The Barrons have invited them to hold the next meeting at the Twin Mountain House. No action can be taken until next January, but it seems quite probable that the next meeting will be held at some point in the mountain region, as many of the teachers would like to avail themselves of the opportunity of visiting the most charming spot in America.

Sylvester Marsh is deserving well of his countrymen for having done so much to make the ascent of Mount Washington so easy and comfortable to all. The Mount Washington railway is certainly an enterprise that has brought joy to the multitude who ascend in its cars to the highest mountain summit in New England. A ride over it is one of those things that cannot be neglected by those who come to the White Mountains. The practical hand of Walter Aiken has made it what it is in completeness and security against accidents.

The Fabyan House is doing a larger business in July than it did last year. It certainly deserves much. It is one of those hotels where everybody feels at home and gets all he pays for. It is fortunate in its central location, and the view of the White Mountain range at sunrise, when tipped with purple and gold, is exceedingly beautiful. No one tires of it. It is in every respect a well-managed hotel, and its reputation is deserved. The Mount Washington railway can be seen from the piazza, with its ascending and descending trains.

Bethlehem is fully alive to the importance of making improvements, trees have been set out in various places and about two miles of plank side walk have been laid. Much of the expense has been borne by the town. The new churches and the new library association, as well as the improvements mentioned above, help to make Bethlehem more attractive to the great number of summer guests who throng the village during the season. It is a good indication, a sign of prosperity that can be made lasting, if each resident will do a little every year to beautify and make attractive.

The Kenney Library Association of Bethlehem has now nearly 500 volumes. It is of recent origin and was brought into existence by those who desire to promote the interests of Bethlehem. Mr. Kenney of Littleton, a former resident, contributed a considerable sum to start the project. Hon. Frank B. Fay of Chelsea gave fifty volumes, and others have also made contributions. The life-membership fee which entitles the donor to a free use of the library, is $5.00. The yearly charge is $1.00. Summer guests are charged two cents a day for the use of books. The library is open three times a week, from two to five, for giving out books.

Among the recent visitors at the Fabyan House were Mr. and Mrs. Samuel Hunt of Boston. Mrs. Hunt visited the mountains thirty-three years ago and stopped at the old Fabyan House, from which she ascended Mt. Washington by the old Fabyan bridle path. The Fabyan cottage now stands where the old Fabyan House stood then. She contrasted the accommodations of that day in the little old red house that would hardly hold fifty people, with the magnificence of the present Fabyan House, and concluded that White Mountain hotel keeping had made rapid strides.

Among the Clouds was issued daily in two editions — one early in the morning and another at 1 PM— and featured news of Mount Washington (including the names of those arriving via the Cog and staying at the Summit House) and the leading White Mountain resort hotels. In addition, many articles of a historical and scientific nature appeared in its pages over the years. To beat the city dailies, the paper was often sent down the mountain on slideboards. Publication ceased in 1908 (see page 96), but the paper was revived and printed at the Cog Railway Base Station from 1910 to 1918.

Built in 1884, the second *Among the Clouds* office contained a fully-equipped printing plant with a Hoe cylinder press and steam engine. Visitors to the summit were encouraged to step inside to view the printing operations.

The Sunset Hill House at Sugar Hill was begun in 1879 and, until it closed in 1973, offered accommodations for three hundred guests and impressive views of Mount Lafayette and the Franconia Range to the south. During this time, tourists had easy access to nearby Franconia Notch via the hotel's fleet of mountain wagons, though many preferred to enjoy the scenery from the hotel's expansive verandas.

73

As a summer resort, few places could rival Bethlehem, NH, in the decades immediately after the Civil War. Word of Bethlehem's beautiful views and healthful climate spread rapidly, thanks in part to an extended visit made in 1863 by Rhode Island Governor Henry Howard. Beginning with the Sinclair House (the large building with the rooftop cupola in the distance), numerous hotels began to spring up along the town's Main Street until there were over thirty places where visitors could choose to spend their summer vacation. Upon the discovery that the town's elevated location brought speedy relief to sufferers of hay-fever, the American Hay-Fever Association adopted the resort community as its headquarters. Regarding this influx of tourism into a town that had once been a sleepy farming community, one White Mountain historian wrote, "The people of the town were, it is said, somewhat slow to appreciate their opportunity, but when, at length, the destiny of the place became evident to them, they were very willing to hasten its development, and provision was made for a water supply, sewer system, and other adjuncts necessary to make the village an attractive place of residence."

An arch covered with greenery awaits the arrival of a coaching parade at Bethlehem's Sinclair House in 1891. One of the largest of the grand White Mountain hotels, the building burned around 1980.

No longer standing, Bethlehem's elegant Upland Terrace hotel, dating from 1877, was made famous in Karl Abbott's 1950 book about White Mountain hotel-keeping, *Open for the Season*.

Named for the prominent nineteenth-century scientist Louis Agassiz, 2,379-foot Mount Agassiz in Bethlehem once sported a summit observatory and carriage road. These well-dressed visitors have stopped next to the tollkeeper's house before making their way up the winding route to the top.

All of the major White Mountain hotels provided musical entertainment for their guests on a regular basis. Swift's Orchestra was in residence at Bethlehem's Maplewood Hotel during the season of 1901. Members were: (from left to right) Walter Johnson, Wiley Swift, Franz Esser, Erich Loeffler, Charles Sharpe, Max Kluge, G. Dana Holt, and William Howard.

Recently renovated, the Maplewood Hotel Casino at Bethlehem once contained bowling alleys, a dance hall, a theater, and facilities for the surrounding golf course, the latter of which is still open to the public. The hotel itself, a towered edifice erected in 1876, stood across the street until 1963.

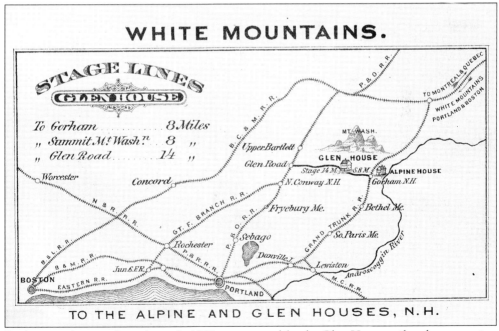

By the time this map from the early 1880s was created for the Glen House, railroad construction had made it possible to leave cities like Boston and Portland in the morning and arrive in time for supper at one of the many popular White Mountain hotels. It took a little longer — about eleven hours — to travel from New York to the same resorts.

Many well-to-do visitors to the White Mountains built substantial "cottages" that now serve as reminders of a time when the region was a playground for the urban elite. The "Wentworth Castle," an elegant Victorian residence at Jackson, NH, was created of local fieldstone for the owners of the nearby Wentworth Hall hotel, which still operates today.

The Iron Mountain House, overlooking the Ellis River at Jackson, NH, was built in 1884 and torn down in the 1940s. Championship tennis tournaments annually brought hundreds of people to this hotel, beginning around 1910. The former hotel annex remains open today under the resort's old name.

The first of four hotels at Jackson, NH, named Gray's Inn, this two-building complex stood from 1885 until 1902. Note the mountain wagon on the right in this White Mountain View Company photograph.

White Mountains, N. H., Grey's Inn, Jackson

The third Gray's Inn at Jackson opened on August 15, 1904, and stood until fire, the great enemy of these large wooden hotels, leveled the building on February 21, 1916. The fourth hotel, a three hundred-room structure that looked much like this one, occupied the same site until just recently.

THE WASHINGTON BOULDER
THORN HILL JACKSON N.H.

A favorite pastime for Victorian-era visitors to the White Mountains was the search for natural profiles in stone of historic American figures. The Washington Boulder in Jackson was one of the better-known examples that drew tourists to the hills.

Reminiscent of the great avalanche that destroyed the Willey family in 1826, the July 1885 "Cherry Mountain Slide" at Jefferson, NH, created a 2-mile path of devastation that wrecked one farmhouse, killed a number of cattle, and "mortally injured" Donald Walker, a local farmhand. Within a few days, special stage excursions were being sent to the site from many of the area's most popular resorts.

The Madison Spring Hut was erected in 1888 by the Appalachian Mountain Club as the first of its many hiking shelters above the treeline. By 1941, when this Shorey Studio photograph was taken, the earlier hut had been replaced by these two facilities.

Despite the coming of the railroads to the White Mountains, stagecoaches continued to be used for short day trips into the mountains. In the 1880s and 1890s, hotel stages, like this one, were elaborately decorated for coaching parades that drew thousands of spectators to such places as Lancaster, Littleton, Bethlehem, and North Conway.

The Crawford Notch Depot on the Portland and Ogdensburg Railroad was erected in 1891. Restored and refurbished, it now serves as an information center operated by the Appalachian Mountain Club.

In the early 1890s the Boston and Maine Railroad extended its tracks from Jefferson Meadow to Berlin, NH, and established the Appalachia station near the Ravine House hotel at Randolph. Although passenger trains no longer travel this route, the spot is an important trailhead for hikers venturing into the northern Presidentials.

The most popular of the three large summer hotels that once stood in the town of Randolph, NH, the Ravine House was long a favorite retreat for a group of mountaineers who, beginning with Lowe's Path in 1875/6, laid out some of the first trails onto the northern Presidentials. The hotel was torn down in 1962.

The former Ravine House swimming pond offered impressive views of Mounts Madison and Adams, as well as rugged King Ravine, from whence the hotel received its name.

Scenes like this, with friendly groups of vacationers rocking away their afternoons on wide hotel verandas, were once commonplace throughout the White Mountains. The porch on the Mount Madison House offered particularly spectacular views of the Carter-Moriah Range of mountains.

One of seventeen logging railroads that once carried millions of feet of timber out of the White Mountains to nearby lumber and pulp mills, the Wild River Railroad operated from 1891 to 1904 in an area straddling the border between Maine and New Hampshire. Shay-type geared locomotives, like the "Gilead," were better able to handle the sharper curves and steeper grades found on many logging railroad lines.

From 1870 to 1948 logging railroads aided in the clearing of some 70,000 acres of forest land in and around the White Mountains. Wrecks, like this one on the Moriah Brook branch of the Wild River Railroad, were frequently caused by improperly laid tracks or mishandled equipment.

Log drives on small streams throughout the White Mountains required tremendous manpower, and many local farmers found a winter's work on these exciting but dangerous operations.

Opportunities for large-scale timber cutting in nearby forests created the city of Berlin, NH, which had become one of the Northeast's major centers of paper production by the turn of the century. The large mill complex shown here, which still functions today, stands very near the site of Dexter Blodgett's Alpine Cascades resort (see page 52), which drew tourists in the 1860s.

This eight-horse Concord coach from the Fabyan House was sent to the summit of Mount Washington on July 20, 1899, to appear in "biograph" pictures. Sponsored by Keith's Theatre in Boston, these early motion pictures of the tallyho stage (the only one of its kind to ever ascend the mountain), the throng at the summit, and the Cog Railway were shown in leading cities in the United States and Europe. The result was a tremendous amount of publicity for Mount Washington

Four

Automobiles
in the Hills

On August 31, 1899, Mr. and Mrs. Freelan O. Stanley, in a steam-powered Locomobile, made the first ascent of Mount Washington by auto in two hours and ten minutes. In 1904, the first of many National Hill Climbing Competitions was held on the "Auto Road" (the name was officially changed from "Carriage Road" in 1911). In 1961, the year of the last auto race, a record of nine minutes thirteen seconds was set for the 8-mile course, much of which is above treeline. This view of the road was taken in the 1920s.

F. W. Rollins, President.   Joseph T. Walker, Secretary.   George T. Cruft, Treasurer.   Philip W. Ayres, Forester.

The Society FOR THE PROTECTION OF New Hampshire Forests

SAVE THE FORESTS

The Society for the Protection of New Hampshire Forests prepared a bill which was passed by the New Hampshire Legislature last winter inviting the Bureau of Forestry at Washington to make a thorough examination of the White Mountain region. This examination is now well under way. The Society desires to use the knowledge thus gained in making an appeal to Congress next winter for a National Forest Reservation in the White Mountains and asks your aid in so doing. The plan has the emphatic endorsement of President Roosevelt, Secretary John Hay, and members of Congress from New Hampshire and other states.

Memberships in the Society are as follows:

Patron Member, - - $100.00
Life Member, - - - - 25.00
Sustaining Member, annually, 10.00
Contributing Member, - - 5.00
Annual Member, - - - 1.00

Checks may be made payable to George T. Cruft, Treasurer, and sent to Bethlehem, N. H., or to 5 Tremont Street, Boston, Mass.

Organized in 1901, the Society for the Protection of New Hampshire Forests was an early and influential leader in pushing for a "national forest reserve" in the White Mountains. Wasteful and destructive lumbering practices in the latter part of the nineteenth century had resulted in public outcries for action, and the Society became an important spokesman for a growing conservation movement in the Northeast.

The *grande dame* of White Mountain resorts, the Mount Washington Hotel at Bretton Woods was first opened to the public on July 28, 1902, the fiftieth anniversary of the opening of the first Summit House atop Mount Washington. This massive, largely wood-framed building (one of the largest in New England) was designed in the then-popular Spanish-Renaissance-Revival-style by the New York architect Charles Alling Gifford, and constructed under the direction of Joseph Stickney, a wealthy New York-based capitalist who had become owner of the nearby Mount Pleasant House in the 1880s. (The nearby Stickney Memorial Chapel, on Route 302, was built in 1906 to honor this ambitious financier who died unexpectedly in 1903.) Standing gracefully on a small ridge some 70 or 80 feet above the surrounding plain, the six hundred-guest hotel was begun in June 1901, and quickly rose to a height of over five stories under the efforts of 250 Italian laborers who were "specialists in carpentry, masonry, and stained glass." The structure's grand ballroom, 900-foot veranda, and exquisite appointments won laurels at the time of its opening. The Mount Washington Hotel was added to the *National Register of Historic Places* in 1978 and has since been designated as a "National Historic Landmark," the highest honor bestowed by the National Park Service, Department of the Interior.

The location of the Mount Washington Hotel in the center of the Ammonoosuc valley not only gave guests impressive views in all directions, but created the impression of a great ship that had somehow come to rest in a spectacular landscape. In the foreground is the hotel's baseball field, and in the background the track of the Mount Washington Cog Railway.

The lobby, or "Assembly Hall," of the Mount Washington Hotel is an impressive interior space that has changed little over the years. In size and elegance, many of the Mount Washington Hotel's rooms compared favorably with the finest of any hotel in the world.

From the beginning, the Mount Washington Hotel catered to motorists, and in 1912, 70 percent of its guests owned automobiles. Whether arriving in their own vehicle or driven by a chauffeur, thousands of guests have enjoyed the fine cuisine in the hotel's huge eight-sided dining room.

The Mount Washington Hotel's "Hemicycle Room" once sported an abundance of wicker furniture and potted plants. The hotel was recently purchased by the owners of the nearby Cog Railway, a move that holds the promise of a safe stewardship into the next century for this priceless monument to an earlier age.

(Left): In 1903 nearly 85,000 acres in northern New Hampshire were destroyed by forest fires, mostly as a result of poor logging procedures and an especially dry season. Soon thereafter, a number of permanent firetowers like this one were erected on peaks throughout the White Mountains as a way of spotting fires early enough to contain them.

(Below): Soon after the completion of a rail line to Fabyans (as the area around the Fabyan House hotel came to be known), a 6-mile branch line was built to Marshfield and opened in June 1876. Before leaving the Fabyan station for the Cog Railway, tourists were often presented with an opportunity to purchase souvenir photographs, such as this example dating from 1904.

The "transfer station" for the Cog Railway and the Fabyan Branch of the Boston and Maine Railroad made it possible to ride, almost uninterrupted, from major cities in the Northeast to the top of Mount Washington. Passenger service from Fabyans to this point was discontinued in 1930 and the tracks were taken up two years later.

The destruction in August 1906 of Fryeburg's only large hotel, the Oxford House, was a blow from which the community's resort business never fully recovered. Most small White Mountain towns lacked the equipment to fight fires in such large wooden buildings.

In 1902 Mount Washington's summit "colony" consisted of a wide variety of buildings and features that often surprised first-time visitors. The identities of the numbered sites above are as follows (number 1 is a Cog Railway train just out of sight at the top): 2. second Summit House; 3. Observation Tower erected in 1880; 4. Tip Top House; 5. printing office of *Among the Clouds*; 6. Carriage Road Stage Office; 7. U.S. Signal Service Station; 8. Railway Engine House; 9. Railway Car Barn; 10. Carriage Road leading down to the Glen and Pinkham Notch; both 11. and 12. stables used by the Carriage Road Company. So attached had New Englanders become to this mountaintop community that few could believe their ears when news arrived of a tremendous fire that, in a few hours, had wiped out what had taken many years to create. As newspapers throughout the country promptly reported, a fire had somehow started in the as-yet-unopened Summit House early on the evening of Thursday, June 18, 1908. With a brisk wind blowing from the west, every summit building, save for the Tip Top House and the two stables (where the gusts lifted burning shingles and clapboards off the roofs before they could catch fire) was soon a mass of flames. As they beheld the smouldering ruins the next day, onlookers agreed it was the end of an epoch for Mount Washington.

Standing like a sentinel over a blackened battlefield, the Summit House chimney is all that remains of the huge two-and-a-half story building. The ancient Tip Top House, on the left, miraculously escaped the conflagration.

Barely discernible in this photograph are the remains of the Signal Station, Carriage Road Stage Office, and Cog Railway Car Barn. Note the remains of the Stage Office stove and chimney.

On the morning of June 19, 1908, all that remained of the former *Among the Clouds* office was its badly damaged Hoe cylinder press and Alamo seven-horsepower engine.

So intense was the heat from the June 1908 fire that the Cog Railway tracks were "twisted into a hopeless mass." In a little over a week, however, trains were again able to run to the top, where a refurbished Tip Top House had been pressed into service to receive that season's visitors.

Constructed in the summer of 1908 to replace an 1878 building destroyed in the Great Fire, the Stage Office atop Mount Washington remained a familiar summit feature until it was razed in August 1976. A similarly constructed office now occupies this site.

An impressive ice storm enveloped Mount Washington for six days in January 1956, producing spectacular scenes such as this of the old Stage Office completely encased in ice measuring from 15 inches to 6 feet in thickness. Such extreme conditions have justifiably given the mountain the characteristic of having "the worst weather on earth."

Named for Senator John W. Weeks of Lancaster, NH, the "Weeks Act" of 1911 permitted the federal government to purchase and set aside large parcels of land to protect important scenic qualities and to conserve valuable natural resources. A product of this turn-of-the-century legislation is the 773,000 acre, 1,200 square mile White Mountain National Forest. The Evans Notch Station, one of several in the National Forest, is located in Bethel, ME.

Fryeburg's picturesque horse railroad was the last of its type to operate in New England. Chartered in 1887 and abandoned in 1913, the 3-mile line ran from the Maine Central Railroad station, up the village Main Street, past the West Oxford Agricultural Fairgrounds, to a popular resort known as Martha's Grove. A portion of the house in the background, which still stands across from Fryeburg Academy, predates 1767, making it one of the oldest in the White Mountain region.

Dixville Notch, at the northern edge of the White Mountains, features a dramatic narrow pass shadowed by knife-edged battlements of granite. A longtime favorite outing for guests at the nearby Balsams hotel has been the climb to Table Rock, in the center of this photograph.

Opened in 1875 as the Dix House, the Balsams hotel at Dixville Notch has been enlarged many times over the years. The man-made Lake Gloriette, which once provided fresh trout for guests' meals, continues to offer swimming and boating opportunities to modern-day visitors.

In 1917, the Balsams hotel was expanded when an eight-story, fireproof wing, shown on the right in this photograph, was constructed. This "bird's-eye-view" was taken from Table Rock, a prominence which lies at the west end of Dixville Notch.

Camping out at the southern end of Dixville Notch in the early 1900s. Though comfortable hotels abounded throughout the White Mountains at this time, many people preferred to experience nature first-hand by immersing themselves in the rustic charms of forest glades like this one.

Mount Washington's third Summit House was begun in 1914 and opened to the public on August 22, 1915. Like the building destroyed by fire in 1908, this heavily-timbered edifice was bolted to the rocks below, and successfully weathered the worst Mother Nature could dish out for over sixty-five years. Besides offering shelter to weary hikers, the hotel continued the mountaintop tradition of providing meals and comfortable overnight accommodations to travelers.

Braced to protect it from the fierce gales that constantly pound Mount Washington's peak, the interior of the third Summit House presents an inviting appearance in this c. 1915 postcard. Note the souvenir stand on the left, the multitude of wooden chairs, and the large framed photograph of the second Summit House over the fireplace.

The warm wood interior of the third Summit House dining room glows in the morning sun in a photograph taken soon after the building opened in 1915. The last regular guests stayed here in 1968.

The effects of World War I were felt in the White Mountain region as well as in the cities of the Northeast. Because many regular employees had enlisted or been drafted, several local hotels ended their season earlier than usual. Mount Washington continued to draw its share of tourists during the conflict, but the Cog Railway did not operate in 1918.

Struck by lightning several times in the nineteenth century, the venerable Tip Top House finally succumbed to fire on August 28, 1915. Soon afterwards, the wooden interior was rebuilt and a stone passageway erected between Tip Top and the Summit House. The original Tip Top House sign is now on display in the Mount Washington Museum on the summit.

A snow-covered and wind-swept Mount Washington looms high above the newly-constructed Eagle Mountain House at Jackson in this 1917 photograph. Renovated as condominiums, this hotel, begun in 1915 and reminiscent of the first Glen House, is a rare survivor from an earlier era.

The Summit Road Company carried passengers to the top of Mount Washington in this fleet of Packard "stages" by the early 1920s. On the right are the Toll House, the third Glen House (once the servants' quarters for the second Glen House), and several large barns.

By the mid-1920s, when this photograph at the Indian Head resort in Franconia Notch was taken, the use of automobiles had caused major changes in travel and tourism in the White Mountains. Cars like these made it possible for less wealthy visitors to tour the region with greater freedom, but they also brought about the decline of the railroads and the grand resort hotels they supported.

Tourist camps, motor courts, and tourist cottages, like these, were built throughout the White Mountains in the 1920s and '30s. By the 1950s, motels began to replace many of these roadside retreats.

The Willey House Camps, in the center of the 6000-acre Crawford Notch State Park, were erected beginning in 1922 and originally included a restaurant, gift shop, and several overnight cabins (now removed) of peeled spruce logs. In this postcard view taken a century after the famous 1826 landslide, the foundation of the old Willey House can be seen at the base of the flagpole on the right.

White Mountains, N. H. Foot of "Tug of War Hill" and Bridge over Silver Cascade.

Early-twentieth-century excursionists found a major challenge in "Tug of War Hill" at the north end of Crawford Notch, above Silver Cascade. A sign here at one time warned auto passengers to "walk up the hill in advance" and drivers to "remain in car to control brakes."

FRED H. DIGBY'S STAND
WHITE MTS. N.H.

Numerous lunch stands and filling stations appeared throughout the White Mountains with the advent of the automobile. The ever-present rack of souvenir postcards (which no doubt included this very photo) rests on Fred Digby's front counter.

The celebrated Eastern Slope Inn in North Conway was built as the Hotel Randall in 1926 and added to the *National Register of Historic Places* in 1982. This impressive Colonial-Revival-style hotel occupies a prominent location on the village's Main Street.

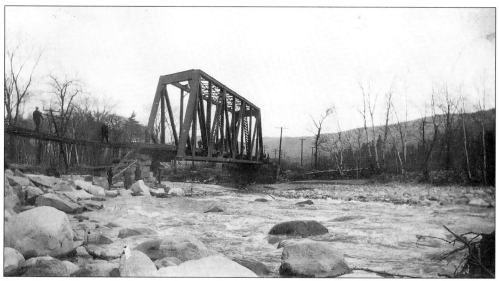

The Grand Trunk Railway bridge at Gorham, NH, was left balancing precariously after floodwaters receded in November 1927. Many communities in the White Mountain region suffered similar damage as a result of this major disaster.

The famous Waumbek Hotel complex at Jefferson, NH, was begun in 1860 by the Plaisted family, and by the turn of the century it had helped to firmly establish Jefferson's superiority as an ideal vacation spot. This interesting pair of towers dominated the west wing of the hotel.

The main road into Jefferson from the east (now Route 2) skirted around part of the Waumbek Hotel before its destruction by fire in 1928. While many of the buildings associated with this resort complex have also disappeared, the hotel's excellent golf course, laid out in 1895, was the first in the White Mountains and has survived intact.

Gorham's Mount Madison House hotel, facing the town common, provided an interesting backdrop for winter fun on the municipal skating rink during the 1920s. Before skiing became the rage, many year-round residents also enjoyed tobogganing, snow-shoeing, and dog-sled racing.

Clark's Trading Post was founded at North Woodstock, NH, in 1928 by Florence M. and Edward P. Clark. Renowned for its trained New Hampshire black bears, this famous White Mountain tourist attraction was originally called "Clark's Eskimo Dog Ranch." On April 3, 1932, Mrs. Clark set a record by becoming the first woman to ascend Mount Washington by dog-sled without assistance.

Clark's Trading Post was the forerunner of the many fun parks and amusement centers now scattered throughout the White Mountains (e.g., Story Land, Santa's Village, Six Gun City, and Heritage New Hampshire). Among its many attractions are a large collection of nickelodeons, an important assemblage of local hotel china, and an excursion ride behind a former logging railroad engine.

The burgeoning popularity of Franconia Notch around the turn of the century resulted in the opening of a new Profile House on July 1, 1906. When a spectacular fire on August 3, 1923, destroyed the hotel, as well as its many cottages and service buildings, the Abbott family, owners of the resort and much of the land around it, decided not to rebuild and instead allowed extensive timber cutting in the area. Outcries over this activity resulted in the purchase of thousands of acres throughout Franconia Notch which were set aside as a "Forest Reservation and State Park" in 1928.

"Old Peppersass," the world's first mountain-climbing cog railway locomotive, was taken out of service in 1878, and later exhibited at major fairs across the country. To commemorate the engine's return and restoration, a special "home-coming" celebration took place on Mount Washington on July 20, 1929. As part of the festivities, which were attended by hundreds of people and numerous dignitaries, engineer E.C. "Jack" Frost, left, and fireman William I. Newsham ran the engine up the mountain as far as the Gulf Tank, above Jacob's Ladder.

"Peppersass" nears the top of Jacob's Ladder during its fateful climb of July 20, 1929. In the process of carrying three extra passengers on its downward journey, the ancient engine suffered mechanical difficulties that caused it to jump the track, killing Daniel Rossiter, an official photographer with the Boston and Maine Railroad, and injuring all the others. Following this tragic event, "Peppersass" was once again restored and returned to Marshfield, where it remains on permanent display.

Created in 1933 during the first term of President Franklin Roosevelt, the Civilian Conservation Corps was one of numerous public works programs designed to put the nation's unemployed back to work. The Cold River CCC Camp at Stow, ME, was one of seventeen similar encampments established in the White Mountain area.

The construction of a highway through scenic Evans Notch, located in the Maine section of the White Mountain National Forest, was just one of many work projects conducted in the 1930s by the Civilian Conservation Corps. Other nearby locations developed by the CCC include the Glen Ellis Falls Scenic Area, the Bear Notch Road, Dolly Copp Campground, the Jewell Trail, and the Hermit Lake Ski Shelters at Tuckerman Ravine.

On April 12, 1934, Mount Washington Observatory staff members Wendell Stephenson, Alexander McKenzie, and Salvatore Pagliuca recorded the highest winds on earth, measuring 231 miles per hour, while huddled inside the old Carriage Road Stage Office. Said one newspaper report of the event, "The Stage Office danced about as much as its heavy chains would permit, and its walls now and then bellowsed in and out."

One of New England's greatest floods inundated towns throughout the White Mountains during March 1936. These men are boating through the village of North Fryeburg where, due to a combination of heavy rain and melted snow, floodwaters from the Saco River isolated local residents for several days.

On September 21, 1938, a hurricane cut a devastating swath across New England. The U.S. Forest Service estimated that enough timber blew down to build two hundred thousand five-room homes. Many locations in the White Mountain area, such as this home and small filling station in Upton, ME, were heavily damaged by falling trees and branches.

New Marshfield House and Mt. Washington, N. H.

The hurricane of 1938 destroyed Jacob's Ladder and a half-mile of trestle on the Cog Railway. With the financial help of Dartmouth College, however, owner Henry Teague soon rebuilt the Railway, adding this log restaurant/souvenir shop and a row of overnight cabins.

The first passenger aerial tramway in North America was built on 4,000-foot Cannon Mountain in 1937/8. In its over forty years of operation, the original tramway carried nearly seven million passengers to the top of this famous peak. The present Cannon Mountain Ski Area also dates back to 1938, when trails were constructed by CCC workers.

4. CANNON MT. AERIAL PASSENGER TRAMWAY FRANCONIA NOTCH, N. H.

The first cars on the Cannon Mountain Aerial Tramway carried twenty-seven passengers and one attendant. "Tram II," which opened in 1980, features a pair of much larger cars capable of holding as many as eighty people each.

The formation of the "Eastern Slope Ski School," inspired by Carroll Reed, and the arrival of ski trains from the Boston area, made North Conway a center of skiing activity in the 1930s. The Skimobile at nearby Mount Cranmore also attracted much attention when it opened in the late 1930s under the enterprising supervision of Harvey Dow Gibson. Though it no longer functions, this unusual conveyance carried hundreds of thousands of skiers and summer tourists to the top of Mount Cranmore over a period of several decades.

Whitney's, at Jackson, NH, began taking in summer boarders before 1900, and by the 1930s offered this modest ski slope where, until 1949, skiers were pulled up the hill by shovel handles. Today, Whitney's is part of the popular Black Mountain winter ski resort.

The city of Berlin was one of many White Mountain communities that established annual winter carnivals in the years before World War II. Often called "Hockey Town," Berlin continues as an active center for winter sports.

Dating back to the 1880s, skiing, and particularly ski jumping, has brought Berlin, NH, great notoriety over the years. Organized competitions by the Nansen Ski Club culminated in 1938 with the construction of this huge ski jump north of the city. Outdated and now falling into disrepair, this North Country landmark may soon become only a memory.

Skiing in the glacial cirque known as Tuckerman Ravine has been a springtime ritual since 1913, and often brings several thousand skiers to Mount Washington's eastern flank well into the month of May. During the 1939 "Inferno" race from the summit to Pinkham Notch, Toni Matt amazed onlookers by "schussing" Tuckerman's Headwall without slowing his speed with the usual turns.

A Bretton Woods landmark for nearly sixty-five years, the 165-room Mount Pleasant House was a much admired Victorian confection that, like many of the grand hotels in the White Mountains, suffered a loss of business during the Depression. As a result, the hotel, a one hundred-room dormitory, the seventy-five-room servant's building, and the central heating plant were demolished in 1939.

Five

The Recent Past

The Mountaineer Leaving Crawford Notch, White Mts., N. H.

World War II brought with it an increase in traffic on railroad routes traversing the White Mountain region, and because much of the freight being hauled was seen as important to the war effort, watchmen were posted near bridges and trestle work to guard against sabotage. Advertised as a "Luxurious, Air-conditioned, Streamlined Train," the 144-passenger, diesel-powered "Mountaineer" (also known as "The Flying Yankee") began running from Boston to Littleton, NH, in 1939, and is seen here emerging from the Great Cut at Crawford Notch in the 1940s. The last regular passenger train service through Crawford Notch took place in April of 1958, and freight service on the Maine Central's Mountain Division ended in the early 1980s.

The "Bretton Woods Monetary Conference" brought international attention to the scenic White Mountains in 1944 when delegates from around the world gathered at the Mount Washington Hotel. For three weeks, starting on July 1st, these representatives met at what was later called the "first 'postwar' conference to be held anywhere in the world."

Winter travel on North Conway's Main Street was sometimes accomplished using dog-sleds previous to the village's transformation into a thriving center for shopping, beginning in the 1960s. Once referred to as the "Eastern Slope," the area surrounding North Conway is now called the "Mount Washington Valley."

The last of the large summer hotels once located in Conway village, the Presidential Inn stood near the junction of Routes 16 and 113, across from the Conway Public Library, until the 1960s. The earliest of the grand hotels in this village was the Conway House, an imposing Greek Revival structure built in 1850 just west of this site.

An era of sorts ended in 1967 when this modest inn, the fourth and last structure in Pinkham Notch to bear the name "Glen House," disappeared in a tragic fire. Though no overnight accommodations are available here today, the spectacular mountain views once enjoyed by nineteenth-century hotel guests still remain for everyone's enjoyment.

The Kearsarge North fire tower, erected in 1951 on a high mountain peak east of North Conway and Intervale, was entered in the *National Historic Lookout Register* in 1991. The original lookout tower on this site was the first in New Hampshire to be equipped using public funds.

Of the grand White Mountain hotels that have disappeared within recent memory, perhaps none were more closely associated with the early history of the region than the famed Crawford House, built in 1859. Changes in travel patterns and the rising costs of operating a large nineteenth-century facility were among the causes for the hotel's closing in 1975. Amid much opposition from many individuals and groups, the contents of the historic hotel were auctioned off in July of 1977. The building itself was destroyed by fire in November of that year.

The Appalachian Mountain Club today maintains hundreds of miles of trails in the White Mountains and continues to perform a leadership role in the areas of conservation and outdoor recreation in the North Country. The Club's Pinkham Notch headquarters was transformed in 1968 when these buildings, dating from the 1920s, were replaced with a new Trading Post, Administration Building, and Joe Dodge Lodge.

The Philbrook Farm Inn, at Shelburne, NH, first opened its doors to guests in 1861 and ranks today as the oldest family-operated hotel in the White Mountains. (The Inn holds additional distinction as the oldest hotel in the United States to be managed by the same family at the same site.) The "Farm," shown here in the 1920s, is located in the picturesque Androscoggin River valley near the Maine/New Hampshire boundary.

The Philbrook Farm Inn mountain wagon, built in 1882, was utilized for many years to transport guests on daily jaunts into the nearby hills and to the top of Mount Washington. In 1896 the wagon was photographed while fording the Androscoggin River at Shelburne. Recently restored, this rare survival from an earlier era of transportation in the White Mountains remains a treasured artifact at the Inn.

Carrying on a White Mountain hotel-keeping tradition first established by the legendary Crawfords early in the nineteenth century, three generations of Philbrooks gathered for this group portrait a number of years ago. Shown are: (standing, left to right) sisters Constance Philbrook Leger, Helen M. Philbrook, and Nancy C. Philbrook; (in front) Ann Leger, Helen Day Philbrook, Lawrence E. Philbrook, and Lawrence P. Leger. The fifth generation of the family now works at the Inn.

One of the most photographed White Mountain locations is the "Shelburne Birches," an area east of Gorham village where a large stand of birch trees crowd the edge of busy Route 2. Now owned by the town of Shelburne, the area has been designated as a living memorial to that community's World War II veterans.

The Mount Washington Auto Road, scene today of annual foot and bike races, continues to uphold its reputation as "America's oldest man-made tourist attraction." An all-time record of nearly forty-five thousand cars ascended the mountain via this road in 1978.

The world's first (and thus oldest) mountain-climbing railroad, the Mount Washington Cog Railway was designated a National Engineering Landmark at a joint meeting of The American Society of Mechanical Engineering and The American Society of Civil Engineering in 1976. The exciting journey to the "top of New England" remains much the same today as when the railway opened 125 years ago.

Recent changes on the summit of Mount Washington have included the restoration of the Tip Top House, at left, and the demolition, in April 1980, of the 1915 Summit House hotel, seen here after it was connected to Tip Top with a stone passageway. The huge steel and concrete Sherman Adams Summit Building now serves as the centerpiece of "Mount Washington State Park," a 60-acre tract established on the mountain top in 1964.

Frozen fog or "rime" shrouds the Mount Washington Observatory building (1937) atop Mount Washington in this Associated Press photograph taken on February 4, 1947. Founded in 1932 and housed since 1980 in the new Sherman Adams Summit Building, the Observatory carries on a tradition of weather measurements and scientific research first established on New England's highest peak during the winter of 1870/1.

In contrast to those parts of the White Mountain National Forest that have been developed over the years for their recreational and commercial potential, certain "Wilderness Areas" have recently been set aside to preserve and protect their fragile environments and outstanding scenic qualities. The 5,552-acre Great Gulf Wilderness, a glacial valley between Mount Washington and the Northern Peaks, received such a designation in 1964. In the background is 5,798-foot Mount Adams.

The Old Man of the Mountain carries on his silent vigil over the White Mountains of Maine and New Hampshire. Since 1916, this world-famous natural wonder has been held to the cliffs of Cannon Mountain with a system of steel rods and turnbuckles, which require annual maintenance. Gazing up at the spectacular profile today, modern visitors can still find inspiration in the oft-repeated quote, attributed to Daniel Webster: "Men hang out signs indicative of their respective trades. Shoe makers hang out a gigantic shoe; jewelers a monstrous watch; even the dentist hangs out a gold tooth; but up in the White Mountains, God Almighty has hung out a sign to show that there He makes men!"